Melody's Songbook of Freedom

Live Your Song LLC

6674 Jr Drive

Kalamazoo, MI 49009

ISBN-13: 978-0-9996630-2-8

To Mya Lov'e Boyd, Shirley Jean Clark, Reverend Eugene E. Hardin, Tashawnya, Darius, Jarius, Rosalyn, Kenny Jr., Raelyn, Darryl, Ryan, Briann, Camille, Austin, Faith, Jah Couri, Javier, Josiah, Elijah, Israel, Kayla, Tangela, Tashawna, Ameriana, Amera, Samaya, Kaitlyn and all the beautiful children of the world.

"Live Your Song" and "Be Free."

You have a choice, choose well.

Now is the time to let your song and voice be heard.

Never Let The Voice Snatchers Steal Your Song,

Lonna Hardin

Ever felt sad? Alone? Afraid?

Have you felt trapped and you needed a way out, but didn't know how?

Black History Month is the time we celebrate great **African American leaders** who felt like this in their own lives.

They still decided to change history and make a big impact on the world.

Black History Month is about the stories and heroes who overcame hardship, pushed through suffering, and each made their mark on the world.

They were champions and victors. What was it that gave them so much strength?

Did you know you also have the power to change things for the better?

You may be wondering how they each made it through hard times.

How did they silence fear and find their voice of freedom?

Music and ***songs*** has always been the key.

Powerful musical sounds that held words of hope for a better life and better land, moved them to defeat the "voice snatchers" in their own lives and look to build a brighter future.

They each hoped for more for their families. They wanted more for future generations and children everywhere.

You can also use ***music*** and ***songs*** to send messages that will change the world and set others free.

In **"Melody's Songbook of Freedom"** Melody travels from helping others escape the "City of the Voice Snatchers" and takes a look at songs from the past that helped pave the way to a "land of freedom" for slaves and helped to end a terrible era in American History.

These songs would give hope to little boys and girls looking for a chance to experience what life is all about.

Let's look at each of the songs that inspired the **"Underground Railroad"** helped slaves escape to a new life, and held hidden codes that led others to the new life they had dreamed.

What are your favorite
songs that make you feel
free?

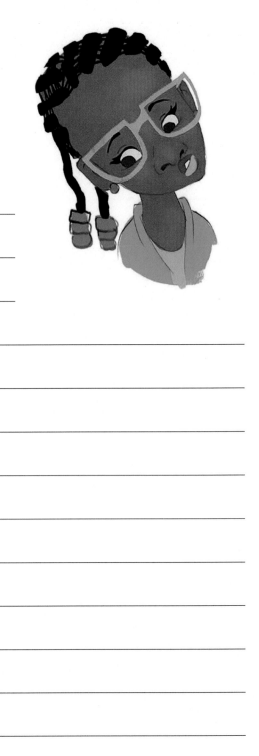

_____

_____

_____

_____

_____

_____

_____

_____

_____

_____

_____

"I freed a thousand slaves. I could have freed a thousand more if only they knew they were slaves."

-- Harriet Tubman

Lift Every Voice and Sing

The Black National Anthem (1900)
Words: James Weldon Johnson
Music: John Rosamond Johnson

Lift every voice and sing, till earth and heaven ring,
Ring with the harmonies of liberty;
Let our rejoicing rise, high as the listening skies,
Let it resound loud as the rolling sea.
Sing a song full of faith that the dark past has taught us,
Sing a song full of hope that the present has brought us;
Facing the rising sun of our new day begun,
Let us march on till victory won.

Stony the road we trod, bitter the chastening rod,
Felt in the days when hope unborn had died;
Yet with a steady beat, have not our weary feet,
Come to the place for which our fathers sighed?
We have come over a way that with tears has been watered,
We have come, treading our path through the blood of the slaughtered;
Out from the gloomy past, till now we stand at last
Where the white gleam of our star is cast.

God of our weary years, God of our silent tears,
Thou who has brought us thus far on the way;
Thou who hast by Thy might, led us into the light,
Keep us forever in the path, we pray.
Lest our feet stray from the places, our God, where we met Thee,
Lest our hearts, drunk with the wine of the world, we forget Thee.
Shadowed beneath Thy hand, may we forever stand,
True to our God, true to our native land.

What do you think life was like for African Americans in 1900?

_____

_____

_____

_____

_____

_____

_____

_____

_____

_____

_____

_____

"If you hear the dogs, keep going. If you see the torches in the woods, keep going. If there's shouting after you, keep going. Don't ever stop. Keep going. If you want a taste of freedom, keep going.

-- Harriet Tubman --

Wade In The Water

Wade in the water
Wade in the water
Wade in the water, children
God is gonna trouble these waters

See that band all dressed in white
God is gonna trouble these waters
It look like a band of the Israelites
God is gonna trouble these waters

See that band all dressed in red
God is gonna trouble these waters
Look like a band that Moses led
God is gonna trouble these waters

My Lord delivered Daniel well
Daniel well, Daniel well
Didn't my Lord deliver Daniel well
Then why not every man?

Man went down to the river
Man went down to the river, Lord
Man went down to the river
Went down there for to pray

Man went down to the river
Man went down to the river, Lord
Man went down to the river
To wash his sins all away

Washed all day, washed all night
Washed till his hands were sore

Washed all day, washed all night
Till he couldn't wash a-no more

(Hey)
Man went down to the river
Man went down to the river, Lord
Man went down to the river
Went down there for to pray

Man went down to the river
Man went down to the river, Lord
Man went down to the river
Washed his sins all away

Wade in the water
Wade in the water, children
Wade in the water
God is gonna trouble these waters

If you don't believe I've been
redeemed
God's gonna trouble the water
Just follow me down to the Jordan's
stream
God's gonna trouble the water.

Wade in the water
Wade in the water, children,
Wade in the water
God's gonna trouble the water

12

Do you know who Harriet Tubman is?

How did she change history?

_____

_____

_____

_____

_____

_____

_____

_____

_____

_____

_____

"I looked at my hands to see if I was the same person. There was such a glory over everything. The sun came up like gold through the trees, and I felt like I was in heaven."

-- Harriet Tubman--

Swing Low, Sweet Chariot
coming for to carry me home

Swing low, sweet chariot,
Coming for to carry me home.
Swing low, sweet chariot,
Coming for to carry me home.

I looked over Jordan, what do I see,
Coming for to carry me home.
A band of angels coming after me,
Coming for to carry me home.

I looked over Jordan, what do I see,
Coming for to carry me home.
A band of angels coming after me,
Coming for to carry me home.

Swing low, sweet chariot,
Coming for to carry me home.
Swing low, sweet chariot,
Coming for to carry me home.

If you could draw this song in a picture, what would it look like?

_____

_____

_____

_____

_____

_____

_____

_____

_____

_____

_____

FUN FACT

Harriet Tubman freed over 300 slaves from Maryland to Pennsylvania.

FOLLOW THE DRINKING GOURD LYRICS

Chorus

Follow the drinking gourd,

Follow the drinking gourd,

For the old man is a-waiting for to carry you to freedom,

Follow the drinking gourd.

Verse 1

When the sun comes back and the first quail calls,

Follow the drinking gourd.

The old man is a waiting for to carry you to freedom,

Follow the drinking gourd.

Chorus

Verse 2

Now the river bank makes a mighty good road,

The dead trees will show you the way.

Left foot, peg foot, traveling on,

Follow the drinking gourd.

Chorus

Verse 3

Now the river ends between two hills,

Follow the drinking gourd.

There's another river on the other side,

Follow the drinking gourd.

Do you think following directions is important? What would have happened if the slaves did not listen to the directions in this song?

_____

_____

_____

_____

_____

_____

_____

_____

FUN FACT

Harriet Tubman (1820-1913)

"The "Moses of her People," Harriet Tubman of the Bucktown District found freedom for herself and some three hundred other slaves whom she led north. In the civil war, she served the Army as a nurse, scout and spy."

Maryland Civil War Centennial Commission

Go Down Moses

Way down in Egypt land

Tell all pharaohs to

Let my people go!

When Israel was in Egypt land

Let my people go!

Oppressed so hard they could not stand

Let my people go!

So the God said: go down, Moses

Way down in Egypt land

Tell all pharaohs to

Let my people go!

So moses went to Egypt land

Let my people go!

He made all pharaohs understand

Let my people go!

Yes the lord said: go down, Moses

Way down in Egypt land

Tell all pharaohs to

Let my people go!

Thus spoke the lord, bold Moses said:

-let my people go!

if not I'll smite, your firstborn's dead

-let my people go!

God-the lord said : go down, Moses

Way down in Egypt land

Tell all pharaohs to

Let my people go!

Tell all pharaohs

To let my people go

Do you know the story of Moses and the children of Israel?

What happened when Pharaoh refused to let them go?

_____

_____

_____

_____

_____

_____

_____

_____

"I had reasoned in my mind, there was one of two things I had a right to, liberty or death; If I could not have one, I would have the other."

--Harriet Tubman--

STEAL AWAY TO JESUS

(Traditional)

Steal away, steal away,
Steal away to Jesus!
Steal away, steal away home,
I ain't got long to stay here.

My Lord, He calls me,
He calls me by the thunder;
The trumpet sounds within my
soul,
I ain't got long to stay here.

Steal away, steal away,
Steal away to Jesus!
Steal away, steal away home,
I ain't got long to stay here.

Green trees are bending,
Poor sinners stand a-trembling;
The trumpet sounds within my
soul,
I ain't got long to stay here.

Steal away, steal away,
Steal away to Jesus!
Steal away, steal away home,
I ain't got long to stay here.

My Lord, He calls me,
He calls me by the lightning;
The trumpet sounds within my
soul,
I ain't got long to stay here.

Have you ever felt like stealing away to a place you loved to be?

Where was it? How did it make you feel every time you went?

_____

_____

_____

_____

_____

_____

_____

_____

"I can say what most conductors can't say-- I never ran my train off the track and I never lost a passenger"

--Harriet Tubman--

The Gospel Train

The Gospel train's comin'
I hear it just at hand
I hear the car wheel rumblin'
And rollin' thro' the land

Get on board little children
Get on board little children
Get on board little children
There's room for many more

I hear the train a-comin'
She's comin' round the curve
She's loosened all her steam and brakes
And strainin' ev'ry nerve

The fare is cheap and all can go
The rich and poor are there
No second class aboard this train
No difference in the fare

Have you ever ridden a
train? How does it sound
when it comes by?

_____

_____

_____

_____

_____

_____

_____

_____

_____

_____

_____

"Life is a hard battle anyway. If we laugh and sing a little as we fight the good fight of freedom, it makes it all go easier. I will not allow my life's light to be determined by the darkness around me."

--Sojourner Truth--

Let Us Break Together

1. Let us break bread together on our knees;
let us break bread together on our knees;
when I fall down on my knees
with my face to the rising sun,
O Lord, have mercy on me.

2. Let us drink wine together on our knees;
let us drink wine together on our knees;
when I fall down on my knees
with my face to the rising sun,
O Lord, have mercy on me.

3. Let us praise God together on our knees;
let us praise God together on our knees;
when I fall down on my knees
with my face to the rising sun,
O Lord, have mercy on me.

Do you have family and
friends you love spending
time with? Who are they?

_____

_____

_____

_____

_____

_____

_____

_____

_____

_____

_____

"I had crossed the line. I was free; but there was no one to welcome me to the land of freedom. I was a stranger in a strange land."

-- Harriet Tubman--

SONG OF THE FREE.

tune—*Susannah*.

I'm on my way to Canada,
   That cold and dreary land,
The dire effects of slavery
   I can no longer stand,
My soul is vexed within me sore
   To think that I'm a slave,
I'm now resolved to strike the blow
   For freedom or the grave.
Oh, righteous father, wilt thou not pity me,
And aid me on to Canada, where colored men are free.

I heard the Queen of England say
   If we would all forsake
Our native land of slavery
   And come across the lake,
That she was standing on the shore
   With arms extended wide,
To give us all a peaceful home
   Beyond the rolling side.
Farewell old master, that's enough for me,
I'm going straight to Canada where colored men are free.

Grieve not my wife,
   Grieve not for me,
Oh, do not break my heart;
   For nought but cruel slavery
Would cause me to depart,
   If I should stay to quell your grief,

Your grief I would augment,
    For no one knows the day that we
Asunder may be rent.
Oh, Susannah don't cry after me,
I'm going up to Canada where colored men are free.

I served my master all my days
    Without a dime's reward,
But now I'm forced to run away
    To flee the lash abhored,
The hounds are baying on my track
    The master just behind,
Resolved that he will bring me back
    Before I cross the line.
Oh, old master don't come after me
I'm going up to Canada where colored men are free.

I heard old master pray last night,
    I heard him pray for me,
That God would come and in his might
    From Satan set me free,
So I from Satan would escape
    And flee the wrath to come,
If there's a fiend in human shape
    Old Master must be one.
Oh, old master while you pray for me
I'm doing all I can to reach the land of liberty.

Ohio's not the place for me,
    For I was much surprised,
So many of her sons to see

In garments of disguise;
Her name has gone throughtout the world
    Free labor, soil and men,
But slaves had better far be hurled
    Into a lion's den.
Farewell Ohio, I'm not safe in thee,
I'll travel on to Canada where colored men are free.

I've now embarked for yonder's shore,
    Where man's a man by law,
The vessel soon will bear me o'er
    To shake the Lion's paw;
I no more dread the auctioneer,
    Nor fear the master's frown,
I no more tremble when I hear
    The baying negro hound.
Oh, old master, don't come after me,
I'm just in sight of Canada, where colored men are free.

I've landed safe in Canada,
    Both soul and body free,
My blood and brains and tears no more
    Shall drench old Tennessee;
Yet I behold the scalding tears
    Now streaming from my eye,
To think my wife, my only dear,
    A slave must live and die.
Oh, Susannah, don't grieve after me,
Forever at the throne of God, I will remember thee.

Many slaves escaped to Canada. What do you think it was like there?

How do you think they felt when they finally made it?

_____

_____

_____

_____

_____

_____

_____

_____

_____

"Every great dream begins with a dreamer. Always remember, you have within you the strength, the patience, and the passion to reach for the stars to change the world."

-- Harriet Tubman --

Now that you've had a chance to learn about some of the music and songs that helped others get through some of the hardest times in Black History, it's your turn.

Take time to write your own song of freedom.

Use it to sing to yourself when you are feeling sad, trapped, or just want to feel free.

Use it to help others and to remind you, you can change the world.

_____

_____

_____

_____

_____

_____

_____

_____

_____

"I'm not going to die. I'm going home like a shooting star."

--Harriet Tubman--

Melody's Songbook of Freedom
Word Search

```
F E B R U A R Y I S B L A C K H I S T O R Y Z M O P E O P L E N T H O T P U Q I
E R F W W C X N B D F M E Z I U L W N B H V N U G O M L X A A I C H E H G D T Z
J N T X E M A Y X D V H O C Q D F L W B A U A M M M S C V D F Q F C A E G O X O
F F H E Y J B N E E T R Z H O K B R E A K K H A U E N W Z O X O B T A L H H N D
A Y R Q D S G C M N G D D Q F I O P Y J W P L Q Z T Y U Y O H L E L V W A W P M
H M I A V W N N A V R Q I D V I J Y V K G G E S K S R Q G C C C U V A R V I I Z
R I D L P Q U A W O H R Z G M K A R D Z C S K L A O I O E N Z Q D B R C D D Y C
U O A Z A J J U T E I P K Y J M V S O R T O B D Q N M T S Z R A Z I L O K R O O
C Q Q Z D T Q B Y C M I M G B I Q T U X I P P Y K G J Q W T K R E Q E G C U V L
X W J N V W J P V O H N C T N N L Y O X Z N K C M I J O J B H T Q U I J D O D P
O N K X Q S R T K U Y E Z Z J F H V S I W L K J T F H I M N I N H P Z J G G N I
O O H B O H D M F N E R R K D A L E R G R K U I S O I N E A O P F Z O G J G U U
R E T A W S K G R X F Y P S K W R U X O F A I A N D V S M T I V I B Q F M W J Q
N C X Q O C T B C Z Q D X U W R W H H W C Q H M Z G L F T I D O E H B V Q O U D
M W G N T U Y T O M V E E V Z O O K J M X E X C M L A G E O I H K Q A U C Z V A
T J G X N J J U Q C L Y D R Y E F Z J N R C L X V O E S L N C I U R F K W U Z X
G S N U T W I B M Q N P D A J P R G L O U F T G V W T R V A X X T U I I Z X L Z
L S T B I Q K M H O O Y Y W W X N U B S F N P F T D S E H L L R G F K F P J W K
O D U G Q E D A F X I Z U B N P U Y I X V D F L Y S T K G Q U Q G D Z Y Q F C M
L T Z U E A H N F E V R L F X G P G G X U M N M C W U A R T V T F S B G H Y G K
C Z D D W I W C T W R M L L F J J G D L Q C C J S M H M H B E V G L M U W K F U
Q D I X S E I Y X X A D P H Q D K X A Q E Z Z O G F Y W X U Z S S P Z U Q U A B
V N F T O E Y O R U Q E H W U S S S I E I C S T X W F A W S O N A I N J L Q D D
N L O U F M G U F W I E O P A R P A I B S I V N T E P N V O R X G A N Y P Y A Z
J R I H F M F R E E D O M M I T L M K I Q J A Q R O U U B B S Y G V K F P S N T
Y K B J T B J U R X F I Y M M R T E C W C B P L P B G T Y P H Y Y E B F G W E P
G T F U C D L B W U P K O R J C S L B X Y Y X N R A X B T I U D P S E S B X V D
P Z Q V Q A L W G Y O G H R G X K O M R Q J N V R L T X P K Z C K A L G S E X F
W S N Y G I T K U X L Y F Z A N A D R R E M Q R J L Z F H I P T X I G Z R P V K
D T E L S B G W P B P F A Y H E Q Y D O I A T N M R V J A U K Y J V K T T M B D
Y F E I E N Q R R X H T S W N B O U J D W S D H P E Z M U S I C Y G Q M X E P O
G A T E I L P R Y Y E O T A P X A H A U I A D P K G C W L V N L K E E W G R T
V J N Z W B H J Y D R O J N Y M O O D K N O U R F G P W F C Z D D C T V N Y R Z
L F T J Y S D E R C F E O C A N N S V K U R U Y E Y U M A F X W Y K R S D U A Q
Y A K L U U I B C P Y F U S R E R N O H R M D G N X D S V A H G O Y D Y A I X A
A Y M O V K U R W Q I M R D Z E W O I X S F T B J G X E W N Y P G V D X U Y S U
O Q U E U C P R S D Y E N V I Y R B C T X P H H O Z L I N G F G A C T R W O Z Q
M K L C O Y Q R U Q Y U E G N I W S E N M O U H G D M C G X A F D A T Z A C R E
Y B T I N G U Q S S L P R C V N N F A J U F A U Q R Z Y B W H S B B B E C E E W D
Y R B R D T G A S R T Z M K S C R N J H Z K S H P N K G Y E Q G D I P P Y S Z V
```

FIND THE FOLLOWING WORDS:

ANTHEM	NATIONAL
AWAY	PEOPLE
BLACK	SNATCHERS
BREAD	SOJOURNER
BREAK	SONG
CHARIOT	SONGS
DRINKING	STEAL
FREEDOM	SWEET
GOURD	SWING
HARRIET	THE
HISTORY	TRUTH
LET	TUBMAN
LOW	VOICE
MAKERS	WADE
MELODY	WATER
MUSIC	

References

"Ella Jenkins – Wade in the Water." *Genius*, genius.com/Ella-jenkins-wade-in-

"Handout 1: Follow the Drinking Gourd Lyrics." *UUA.org*, 20 July 2017, www.uua.org/re/tapestry/children/loveguide/session15/169036.shtml.

"Go Down Moses." *Wikipedia*, Wikimedia Foundation, 27 Jan. 2018, en.wikipedia.org/wiki/Go_Down_Moses.

Hymnlyrics.org, www.hymnlyrics.org/hymns_spirituals/the_gospel_train.php.

"Lift Every Voice And Sing (The Black National Anthem)." *The Black National Anthem | The Black Past: Remembered and Reclaimed*, BlackPast.org Staff, www.blackpast.org/special/black-national-anthem.

Lyrics for Hymn #548, 'Let Us Break Bread Together', www.pateys.nf.ca/cgi-bin/lyrics.pl?hymnnumber=548.

"Song of the Free." *Wikipedia*, Wikimedia Foundation, 22 Jan. 2018, en.wikipedia.org/wiki/Song_of_the_Free.

"STEAL AWAY TO JESUS (Traditional) ." *STEAL AWAY TO JESUS - Lyrics - International Lyrics Playground*, lyricsplayground.com/alpha/songs/s/stealawaytojesus.shtml.

Made in the USA
Middletown, DE
20 January 2019